HELIBORNE

USMC HELICOPTER ASSAULT

HELIBORNE

USMC HELICOPTER ASSAULT

Yves Debay with Lindsay Peacock

OSPREY
AEROSPACE

First published in Great Britain in 1993
by Osprey, an imprint of
Reed Consumer Books Limited
Michelin House, 81 Fulham Road,
London SW3 6RB
and Auckland, Melbourne, Singapore and
Toronto

ISBN 1 85532 311 7

Edited by Tony Holmes
Page design by Paul Kime
Printed in Hong Kong

Front cover Cruising at 2000 ft above the frozen tundra of northern Norway, a well-weathered CH-46E from HMM-263 heads back towards USS *Guadalcanal* after depositing a squad of Marines in the *Team Work 92* exercise area. Although this newish grey scheme suits the climatic conditions experienced in the Arctic circle, it tends to expose the helicopter's susceptibility to fluid leaks and the general weathering of open deck life whilst on cruise

Back cover The bolt-on refuelling probe sturdily attached to this CH-53E has been liberally adorned with high-viz masking tape so as to make it clearly visible to aircraft handlers on the crowded deck of *Guadalcanal*. The probes are usually only fitted during exercise periods when the USMC make a KC-130 tanker available for inflight refuelling – most of the time whilst on deployment the helicopter carrier will be out of tanker range

Title page Affectionately referred to as the 'frog' – an allusion to its highly distinctive frontal aspect – Boeing-Vertol's Sea Knight has been a stalwart of Marine Corps rotary-winged aviation since as long ago as June 1964, when the first production examples of the CH-46A model were delivered to Medium Helicopter Squadron (HMM) -265 at New River, North Carolina. Eventually entirely replacing the 1950s-vintage UH-34 Seahorse, progressive updating of the Sea Knight resulted in the present day CH-46E, which now equips no fewer than 14 frontline squadrons

For a catalogue of all books published by Osprey Aerospace
please write to:

**The Marketing Department, Reed Consumer Books,
1st Floor, Michelin House, 81 Fulham Road, London SW3 6RB**

Guided by a member of the flightdeck crew, a CH-46E Sea Knight is silhouetted against the dusk as it lifts off from its floating home and heads for the beach during a routine amphibious assault exercise. In the background another 'frog' and a CH-53E Super Stallion spin up to full power as they await orders to launch. Marine Corps vertical envelopment operating doctrine is dependent upon these two types bearing the brunt of the resupply effort once the troops have gone ashore and secured a beach-head

Introduction

Events in the recent Gulf War confirmed, if ever confirmation was needed, that the helicopter is now an essential weapon of war, whether it be in overtly aggressive roles such as the destruction of armoured fighting vehicles or in boosting mobility by moving men and equipment around the battlefield.

It was not always thus, of course, and it took some considerable time for the unique qualities of the helicopter to be fully accepted and, perhaps more importantly, fully exploited. Much of the credit for that achievement can be laid firmly at the door of the US Marine Corps, an agency that first experimented with rotary-winged craft some 61 years ago when it evaluated the Pitcairn OP-1 autogyro at Quantico, Virginia, and in Nicaragua during the course of 1932.

Those early trials actually proved far from satisfactory and Marine Corps interest fell into a dormant state until June 1946 when the service formally established a helicopter programme. Tangible evidence of this came in December 1947 with the creation of HMX-1, a unit that was tasked specifically with exploring the potential of helicopters and possible Marine Corps applications. The trail-blazing activities of HMX-1 also extended to the development of operational tactics and paved the way for the first combat employment, which occurred in 1951 when observation helicopters like the Sikorsky HO5S and transport machines such as the Sikorsky HRS saw action in the Korean War.

Today, those primitive machines are long gone, but the traditions established in the battlefields of Korea – and, a decade or so later, in war-torn Vietnam – are well remembered by the lineal descendants of those pioneering units. As for the helicopter itself, this continues to play a major role in Corps service. Some of the missions may have changed little in so far as the objectives are concerned, but the contemporary turbine-powered Sea Knights and Super Stallions are infinitely more capable and reliable items of hardware.

Helicopter evolution has by no means been limited to the creation of bigger and better cargo-haulers and one worthwhile development that arose directly as a result of the war in Vietnam is the armed and armoured 'gunship'. Not surprisingly, the Marine Corps was quick to recognise the potential and deploy armed helicopters of its own, but new weapons have resulted in the simple 'gunship' being transformed into a lethal 'tank-buster' that is perhaps best epitomised by the SuperCobra, a type that employed its TOW and Hellfire anti-armour missiles to quite deadly effect in the Gulf.

Along with the utilitarian Iroquois, these three very different types constitute the backbone of today's Marine Corps helicopter force and all of them feature prominently in the pages that follow, so join us now in a closer exploration of a world that includes such esoteric creatures as 'pigs' and 'frogs' and is peopled by such strange sounding individuals as 'leathernecks' and 'grunts'.

Right Temporary structures and desert-camouflaged helicopters provide clues that this UH-1N Iroquois of HMLA-367 was one of a number deployed to Saudi Arabia as part of the massive US contribution to the liberation of Kuwait. Door-mounted M60 7.62 mm machine guns offer a measure of self-protection and one that might well be of value since the Huey is often tasked with scouting for the more potent AH-1 Cobra gunships. Other missions include utility combat support and medical evacuation, while it may also assist with the movement of supplies and equipment from ship to shore

Contents

Tank Killer 8

Heavy Lift 30

The Workhorse 52

The veteran Huey 94

Desert Shield 104

Marine Helicopter Squadrons 128

Tank killer

Different colour schemes and different armament configurations are apparent on this pair of AH-1T SeaCobras at a helicopter landing site at Canjuers, France, in January 1990. In line with normal Marine Corps practice when operating from an amphibious assault vessel, they have been assigned to a composite helicopter squadron. Such units are organised specifically for sea-based operations and generally utilise a Medium Helicopter Squadron as the 'core unit'. They will direct the activities of a disparate collection of types that might include examples of the SeaCobra or SuperCobra, the Iroquois, the Sea Knight and the Sea Stallion or Super Stallion

Left A SeaCobra gunner gives the photographer a friendly thumbs-up signal before departing for a 'play area' during an exercise somewhere in the south of France. This view emphasises well the narrow frontal aspect of the SeaCobra fuselage, and also shows the stub wings on which can be carried an impressive array of weaponry. Ordnance options include Sidewinder heat-seeking air-to-air missiles, TOW wire-guided anti-tank missiles and unguided rockets, while the triple barrels of the integral turret-mounted XM-197 20 mm cannon are also evident

Above A 'twin-pack' TOW missile installation is carried by this AH-1T although no armament is actually fitted. Marine Corps procurement of the AH-1T totalled 55 but almost all of these have since been upgraded to the even more capable AH-1W SuperCobra standard. Half-a-dozen frontline light attack squadrons and a training outfit presently utilise the definitive AH-1W version of Bell's potent gunship, attack helicopter resources being rounded out by two second-line units of the Marine Corps Reserve, which have recently replaced their AH-1J models with the AH-1W

Left The black, grey and green disruptive camouflage applied to this SeaCobra might well be effective in cutting down the risk of observation by unwanted eyes but it certainly does not mask the fact that this mean machine is far from being aesthetically pleasing. But 'handsome is as handsome does', and it cannot be denied that the SeaCobra and the SuperCobra are indeed admirable exponents of the lethal art of tank-busting

Above Although the US Army were the driving force behind the initial development of the helicopter gunship concept, much of the responsibility for subsequent improvement initiatives rests with the Marine Corps, which has operated four different versions over the years. The first of these was the AH-1G, which began to enter service in February 1969, making its combat debut in Vietnam in April of the same year. These initial aircraft were actually diverted from Army contracts on a loan basis, but acquisition of the first purpose-built AH-1J SeaCobras occurred in July 1970 and they have since been followed by the much more heavily armed AH-1T and AH-1W, with the latter now being the most widely used sub-type. Including the loaned machines, total procurement for the Marine Corps eventually exceeded 250

'Don't look now, but I think we're being followed.' A gunner stares back from his cockpit as the SeaCobra in which he is flying is pursued across the south of France by a camera ship. The closely-cowled exhaust nozzles of the AH-1T version are particularly evident in this unusual view, while this machine is also fitted with an infrared jamming device on the upper surface of the engine bay, directly behind the main rotor shaft. Active countermeasures equipment, in the form of flare dispensers, are also mounted on the top of the stub wings

Bell AH-1T

Rotor system: main rotor diameter 48 ft 0 in (14.63 m) tail rotor diameter 9 ft 8.5 in (2.96 m); main rotor disc 1809. 56 sq ft (186.11m²); tail rotor disc area 74.02 sq ft (6.88 m²)

Wing: span 10 ft 4 in (3.15 m)

Fuselage and tail: length overall, rotors turning 56 ft 11 in (17.35 m) and fuselage 45 ft 6 in (14.68 m); height overall 13 ft 6.25 in (4.12 m)

Powerplant: one Pratt & Whitney Canada T400-WV-402 rated at 1970 shp 1469 kW

Weights: empty 8014 lb (3635 kg); operating empty 8608 lb (3904 kg); maximum take-off 14,000 lb (6350 kg)

Fuel and load: internal fuel 304.5 US gal (1153 litres) external fuel up to four 77-US gal (291-litre) or two 100-US gal (378-litre) external tanks; maximum useful load (fuel and ordnance) 5392 lb (2445 kg)

Speed: never exceed 207 mph (333 km/h); maximum level speed 'clean' at sea level 172 mph (277 km/h)

Range: maximum range 359 miles (577 km)

Performance: maximum rate of climb at sea level 1785 ft (544 m) per minute; service ceiling 7500 ft (2255 m)

Above A member of the ship's company loosens the tie-down chains which secure a particularly ferocious-looking HMM-365 AH-1T SeaCobra to the flight deck of the USS *Iwo Jima* (LPH-2) during operations with the US 6th Fleet in the Mediterranean Sea. In the background, another gunship from the same unit decelerates to a hover and awaits its turn to recover in the spot that will soon be vacated

Right Clad in combat fatigues, a technician gets down to work on a SeaCobra gun turret that, somewhat unusually, has been decorated with a shark-mouth motif. Nose-mounted sensors associated with weapon aiming sub-systems are visible while the item protruding from the side of the nose is one of four radar warning receivers fitted to the AH-1T. Located in pairs on either side of the nose and tailboom, these devices bestow full hemisphere coverage, with crew members being alerted to hostile radars by audible warnings as well as a cockpit display which indicates the range and bearing of the emitter that is 'painting' them

Left 'Yup, that looks all right to me.' Wearing the almost obligatory dark glasses but lacking a unit insignia shoulder patch, a Cobra driver peers closely at the complex collection of moving parts which comprise the rotor head assembly. Failure of any one of these components could very quickly transform a nice day into a nasty one, so it is hardly surprising that he takes care to confirm to himself that all is in order. The flat plate visible on the left is the anchor point for an infrared jamming device

Above Lush green vegetation provides a stark contrast to the rocky outcrops in the distance as an AH-1T SeaCobra cruises by, but do not be fooled by the apparent serenity of this scene. Although the TOW-configured helicopter stands out clearly against the sky from this low observation point, it is almost certainly taking full advantage of the plentiful tree cover to mask its approach from 'hostile' forces playing the 'bad guys' in a training exercise. In a real shooting match, the first warning that a distant column of tanks and other armoured fighting vehicles might expect to get is when the missiles start impacting in the target area

Far and away the most potent of the navalised gunships, the AH-1W is most easily recognised by its revised engine efflux outlets, these being markedly larger than those of the AH-1J and AH-1T. Although this particular example of the 'Whisky' Cobra carries a TOW missile installation, the AH-1W is compatible with the newer and potentially much more lethal Hellfire anti-armour missile, a weapon that achieved conspicuous success in the Gulf War. The presence of a mobile mirror landing system in the background indicates that even helicopter pilots have to undergo field carrier landing practice as part of routine peacetime training

Bell AH-1W

Rotor system: main rotor diameter 48 ft 0 in (14.63 m); tail rotor diameter 9 ft 9 in (2.97 m); main rotor disc 1809.56 sq ft (168.11m^2); tail rotor disc area 74.70 sq ft (6.94m^2)

Wing: span 10 ft 7 in (3.23 m); aspect ratio 3.74

Fuselage and tail: length overall, rotors turning 58 ft 0 in (17.68 m) and fuselage 45 ft 6 in (13.87 m); height overall 14 ft 2 in (4.32 m) and to top of rotor head 13 ft 6 in (4.11 m); tailplane span 6 ft 11 in (2.11 m)

Powerplant: two General Electric T700-GE-401 rated at 1690 shp (1260 kW)

Weights: empty 10,200 lb (4627 kg); maximum take-off 14,750 lb (6690 kg)

Fuel and load: internal fuel 304.5 US gal (1153 litres); external fuel up to four 77-US gal (291-litre) or two 100-US gal (378-litre) external tanks; maximum ordnance 2466 lbs (1119 kg)

Speed: never exceed 219 mph (352 km/h); maximum level speed 'clean' at sea level 175 mph (282 km/h); cruising speed at optimum altitude 173 mph (278 km/h)

Range: range at sea level with standard fuel 395 miles (635 km)

Performance: maximum rate of climb at sea level, one engine out 800 ft (244 m) per minute; service ceiling more than 12,000 ft (4495 m) in ground effect

Left Pre-flight routines performed by the SeaCobra pilot and gunner differ quite significantly, but both are essential if the task is to be conducted efficiently and successfully. Here, a gunship pilot aboard *Iwo Jima* busies himself with checking the physical condition of his mount, while his gunner confirms that he has the necessary maps and paperwork relating to the target area in which they will soon be working. In a matter of minutes, they will occupy their respective cockpits and undertake more checks before clattering away from the ship

Above Deck crew members perform last-minute checks on a pair of HMM-365 AH-1T SeaCobras which sit with their engines idling as they await orders to launch from *Iwo Jima* during joint military operations with French forces in the south of France. Even though it is perfectly possible for combat operations to be conducted from ships at sea for sustained periods, the service chiefs are well aware that such vessels make attractive targets and Marine operating doctrine does anticipate establishing shore facilities as soon as possible in order that these valuable helicopters can be dispersed among less vulnerable sites

'We surrender!' Pilot and gunner of an AH-1T SeaCobra take full advantage of a brief lull in rather more serious business to indulge in a bit of horseplay for the photographer's benefit. Moments later, all thoughts of humour are forgotten as they lift off and head out towards the 'play area' which lies conveniently close to the forward operating location at Canjuers. Even though this is just another in a long string of exercises, and despite the fact that this AH-1T is not carrying such potent tank-busting weapons as TOW and Hellfire, there is nothing to prevent the gunner from using his sighting aids to find and, theoretically at least, destroy 'hostile' armour

Marine Corps helicopters are a perennial feature of the NATO *Team Work* exercise which traditionally takes place in northern waters and which regularly involves a full-blown amphibious assault landing in Norway. In early 1992 the USS *Guadalcanal* (LPH-7) was one of the vessels involved. Seen here in a Norwegian fjord against an imposing backdrop of snow-clad mountains, *Guadalcanal* prepares to launch a gaggle of helicopters which will be led into action by a pair of AH-1W SuperCobras tasked with 'sanitising' the landing zone

Above Maximising the impact of an attack is probably the name of the game as far as anti-armour combat operations are concerned and it is reasonable to assume that Marine Corps gunships would operate in groups rather than singly. This would allow them to engage multiple targets with a salvo of missiles, each gunship probably firing no more than two weapons at different objectives before withdrawing from the killing ground in order to prepare another ambush at a different, but still tactically favourable, location. Routine training would certainly entail the use of tactics that would be employed in battle. These two SeaCobras are returning to refuel before rejoining the 'fight' while on exercise in France

Right If the SeaCobra is to stand any chance of being successful in its task, it is vital for both crew members to work as a team. In the final analysis though, much still depends on the skill of the gunner, whose task it is to aim and guide weapons like the TOW missile to their targets. While the gunner's 'office' is clearly dominated by high-tech kit such as the sighting device seen here, there is also scope for rather more basic equipment and even the humble map still has an important part to play in the successful execution of anti-armour operations

Heavy-lift

If the SeaCobra and SuperCobra can be referred to as the 'sports cars' of Marine Corps helicopter aviation forces, then the mighty Sikorsky CH-53E Super Stallion certainly merits being known as the 'pantechnicon', if only by virtue of its almost unparalleled lifting capability. Whether it be fully-equipped troops or, as seen here, heavy equipment, most loads come easy to the Super Stallion, but the sheer bulk of this machine perhaps disguises the fact that it has an important part to play in enhancing mobility. Certainly, its ability to shift items such as field artillery pieces from one firing point to another is of vital assistance in allowing the Marines to conduct a swiftly moving war in terrain that can vary from desert plains to mountainous regions, and encompassing virtually everything in between

Carrying externally slung loads might be a commonplace event but it is certainly not an activity that is undertaken lightly, if you will forgive an unintentional pun. There are many pitfalls to trap the unwary and even though the Super Stallion's triple-engine layout gives the pilot bags of power in reserve, considerations such as weight and balance must be determined and adhered to if a hoist is to be accomplished safely and efficiently. These two views portray a CH-53E preparing to move an artillery piece to a new firing location, the down-draught from that massive seven-bladed main rotor making life more than a little difficult for the unfortunate individuals whose job it is to hook up the load in readiness for a lift

With the underslung load secure, a CH-53E climbs away from the collection point and sets course towards its destination, which lies no more than a dozen miles away. Transit to the new firing site takes minutes rather than the hours that would be needed if the weapon had to be dragged across country by a truck, and unloading is the work of moments. With other helicopters being used to airlift in fresh stocks of ammunition, the artillery piece can quickly be brought back into action in support of ground forces intent on maintaining the impetus of an offensive operation. There are some who might remark that the CH-53E is a rather expensive gun carriage but this is only a typical example of the type of load that can be carried externally, and one has only to look back at the Vietnam War to appreciate just how sound an investment the heavy-lift helicopter can be. Then, in barely four months of operations by the first four CH-53As deployed to South-east Asia, no fewer than 103 aircraft and helicopters were recovered, many of which would certainly have been lost as a result of enemy action had it not been for the presence of the Sea Stallion

Sikorsky CH-53E

Rotor system: main rotor diameter 79 ft 0 in (24.08 m); tail rotor diameter 20 ft 0 in (6.10 m); main rotor disc area 4901.7 sq ft (455.38 m²); tail rotor disc area 314.2 sq ft (29.19 m²)

Fuselage and tail: length overall, rotors turning 99 ft 0.5 in (30.19 m), fuselage 73 ft 4 in (22.35 m), and overall with rotor and tail pylon folded 60 ft 6 in (18.44 m); height overall, rotors turning 29 ft 5 in (8.97 m), to top of rotor head 17 ft 5.5 in (5.32 m), and overall with rotor and tail pylon folded 18 ft 7 in (5.66 m); wheel base 27 ft 3 in (8.31 m)

Powerplant: three General Electric T64-GE-416 rated at 4380 shp (3266 kW) for 10 minutes, 4145 shp (3091 kW) for 30 minutes and 3696 shp (2756 kW) for continuous running

Weights: empty 33,228 lb (15,072 kg); maximum take-off 69,750 lb (31640 kg) with an internal payload or 73,500 lb (33,340 kg) with an external payload

Fuel and load: internal fuel 1017 US gal (3849 litres); external fuel up to two 650-US gal (2461-litre) drop tanks; maximum payload 36,000 lb (16,330 kg), or 30,000 lb (13,607 kg) carried internally over a 115-mile (185-km) radius or 32,000 lb (14,515 kg) carried externally over 57.5-mile (92.5-km) radius

Speed: maximum level speed 'clean' at sea level 196 mph (315 km/h); cruising speed at sea level 173 mph (278 km/h)

Range: ferry range without aerial refuelling 1290 miles (2075 km) radius 575 miles (925 km) with a 20,000-lb (9072-kg) external payload or 57.5 miles (92.5 km) with a 32,000-lb (14515-kg) external payload

Performance: maximum rate of climb at sea level with a 25,000 lb (11340 kg) payload 2500 ft (762 m) per minute; service ceiling 18,500 ft (5640 m); hovering ceiling 11,550 ft (3520 m) in ground effect and 9500 ft (2895 m) out of ground effect

Drab green camouflage cannot disguise the fact that the CH-53E Super Stallion is big and bulky, and even the most ardent supporter of Sikorsky's heavy-lifter is hardly likely to claim that it ranks amongst the more attractive helicopters that can be seen today. That is one reason why it is affectionately referred to as the 'pig', although another factor might well relate to its ability to pack in more 'grunts' than any other helicopter in the Marine Corps inventory, for it can accommodate no fewer than 56 foot soldiers. Alternatively, when employed on cargo-carrying operations, it is able to hoist an impressive 32,000 lb payload, although fuel restrictions limit the radius to approximately 50 miles. In-flight refuelling from Marine Corps KC-130 Hercules tanker aircraft could, in theory, extend that range, but such a concept is most likely to be used during deployment when it might well be desirable to boost the helicopter's 1000-nautical mile ferry range. In these two studies of a CH-53E flying just off the French Mediterranean coast, the in-flight refuelling probe is clearly visible and this will be extended still further for refuelling so as to eliminate the chance of the rotor blades being fouled by a tanker's hose-and-drogue

Above Although it bears a strong family resemblance to earlier models, the CH-53E is sufficiently different from its predecessors as to fully merit the adoption of the name Super Stallion. One of those differences is certainly evident here, for the Echo version has a seven-bladed main rotor, unlike the CH-53A and CH-53D, both of which relied on just six blades. Entering service as long ago as the autumn of 1966, the CH-53A was intended to replace the CH-37 Mojave as the prime heavy-lift vehicle and well over 100 were completed for the Marines before production turned to the CH-53D which had an enlarged cabin and more powerful engines. Today, the original CH-53A has all but disappeared from the scene, but the CH-53D is still active with four frontline squadrons as well as a training unit and Reserve force elements. However, it is the CH-53E which is now the most widely used version of the Stallion, and this presently serves with five regular Marine Corps outfits as well as elements of the Navy. The two Super Stallions shown here in landing configuration are typical of the breed

Left Apart from a two-digit code number on the extreme nose section, this CH-53E appears to be virtually anonymous, its dark green paint job offering little or no contrast to the black national insignia and other markings. Caught as it flares for landing at a forward operating location in the south of France, the Super Stallion is actually assigned to HMM-365 which was embarked on *Iwo Jima* for a spring cruise in 1988

The unit marking visible directly above the cockpit of this Super Stallion provides confirmation that it was temporarily on the strength of HMM-162 when deployed to Corsica in early 1989. Rather unusually, the nose-mounted in-flight refuelling probe has been deleted, although the attachment point is clearly apparent in this striking view of a 'pig' as it prepares to undertake an external lift operation. Thicker than the average individual's wrist, the cable employed for the carriage of externally slung cargo can be seen dangling through the 'hell-hole' under the centre fuselage section and it is usual for at least one member of crew to monitor the load from this position throughout a vertical lift. In the event of any problems arising, a quick-release mechanism allows the load to be hastily jettisoned in order to ensure the safety of helicopter and crew

In addition to the differences alluded to earlier, the CH-53E features several other noteworthy changes when compared with older models. Foremost among these has been the switch from a twin to a three-engined layout, which, in conjunction with improved transmission units, offers much higher levels of operating safety as well as a much enhanced heavy-lift capability. Perhaps less significant, but rather more obvious, is the revised tail configuration introduced as a result of testing a pair of YCH-53E prototypes. On those machines, the layout used initially comprised an upright vertical fin with two low-set horizontal surfaces but the production Super Stallion eventually appeared with a tail rotor pylon that is quite noticeably canted to port, as well as a high-set gull-wing horizontal surface that relies on a bracing strut for additional strength

Above While it cannot honestly be referred to as travelling in style, there is no doubt that being airlifted to a landing site in one's jeep is certainly a very different way of setting off for a drive in the French countryside. In the gloom of the cabin, another jeep is about to be driven clear, after which the CH-53E will head back out to *Iwo Jima* for a fresh load

Right Three Super Stallions, half-a-dozen Sea Knights and a brace of SeaCobras are pictured on the landing site at Canjuers in May 1988 as they take full advantage of the respite offered by a lull in HMM-365's flying programme. Normally used by helicopters of the French Army, the landing spots at Canjuers clearly were not laid out with the much larger Marine Corps machines in mind. Nor, it appears, is the maintenance set-up quite as well organised as that on board the parent vessel, if the rather 'Heath-Robinsonish' method of gaining access to the tail rotor of the Super Stallion in the centre of the picture is anything to go by

Three-tone camouflage was applied to at least two of the CH-53E Super Stallions that were embarked aboard *Iwo Jima* as part of HMM-365 in early 1990 and at least one also carried an additional (and probably unofficial) extra marking in the form of a Superman logo directly above the cockpit. These two views portray flightdeck activity on *Iwo Jima* during amphibious assault training operations conducted off the coast of France. In the best of conditions – which these certainly are not – a flight deck is a potentially lethal environment in which to work, but a rain-slick and greasy landing platform must surely increase the dangers faced by the landing officer seen here, especially in view of the down-draught generated by the Super Stallion

Near cloudless skies and a brilliantly blue sea are much more the sort of weather conditions that one normally associates with the Mediterranean and they were certainly much in evidence in these two studies of Super Stallions awaiting the order to lift off from *Iwo Jima*. Although the CH-53E and its nickname of 'pig' might well convey an impression of being ponderous and ungainly, appearances are assuredly deceptive in this instance, for it does possess a fairly nifty turn of speed and is quite capable of zipping along at an impressive 196 mph. Even more remarkable, though, is its agility, with some members of the Stallion family having performed loops and rolls. Ultimately, though, it is as a load carrier that it works best and the current CH-53E version has demonstrated the ability to lift an impressive 93 per cent of the heavy equipment in a typical Marine divisional organisation. When one recalls that its immediate predecessor, the CH-53D, could only hoist a modest 38 per cent, the value of the Super Stallion to the Marine Corps is all too readily apparent

Few helicopters can be quite as well suited for humanitarian and disaster relief missions as the CH-53E. Whether the nature of the task is that of airlifting people to sanctuary or the movement of supplies such as food and shelter, the Super Stallion's payload capability combines with its 'go-anywhere' potential to permit just a handful of machines to achieve rather more than is possible with conventional fixed-wing aircraft. That capability was certainly put to one of its sternest tests in operation *Provide Comfort*, when aircraft and helicopters that had been embroiled in the Gulf War just a few weeks earlier turned their attentions to bringing succour to Kurdish refugees fleeing from Saddam Hussein's genocidal activities in northern Iraq. Such work was accomplished in the face of occasional opposition from Iraqi troops, hence the need for allied fighter cover and the decision to retain defensive machine gun armament on the Super Stallions *(Both photographs by Patrick Allen)*

The workhorse

Staying with the motoring comparisons, Boeing-Vertol's long-serving Sea Knight conceivably merits being described as the 'pick-up truck' in Marine Corps service. While it certainly cannot match the Sea Stallion or Super Stallion in sheer lifting ability, it has not earned the appellation workhorse for nothing. So, whether it be bullets or beans and sleeping bags or soldiers, the Sea Knight has repeatedly demonstrated that it is more than equal to the task. Here, amidst a cloud of spray whipped up by its tandem rotor blades, a CH-46E Sea Knight from HMM-162 is seen in typical nose-high landing attitude just seconds before it hits the beach while demonstrating vertical envelopment techniques

A third Sea Knight sweeps in to land as a pair of CH-46Es prepare to lift off after depositing troops on the newly established beach-head. Within moments, they will be heading back out to the parent vessel some distance offshore to collect a fresh cargo. It might be extra Marine 'grunts' to consolidate the position during the vulnerable early stages of an assault landing, or some of the equipment that will be needed by land-based forces as they attempt to break out from their precarious toe-hold on 'enemy' territory. More than 40 years of helicopter operations have allowed the US Marine Corps to develop and hone such skills to near perfection, but despite their expertise and a wealth of exposure to the hazards of battle, there have not really been all that many opportunities to test vertical envelopment assault skills in combat

Three-tone black, green and grey camouflage fails to disguise the distinctive shape of the Sea Knight as two more examples from HMM-162 decelerate and descend for touch-down, recreating a scene that has been enacted countless times since Boeing-Vertol's versatile helicopter began to enter the Marine Corps inventory in the early 1960s

Above Progressive development of the Sea Knight by the manufacturer resulted in three major versions being delivered to the Marine Corps, specifically the CH-46A, CH-46D and CH-46F, but most surviving examples were subsequently modernised to the CH-46E standard during the 1980s and this version is now active with all first and second-line medium helicopter squadrons. Updating basically entailed a switch to a more powerful version of the General Electric T58 turboshaft engine and provision of increased crash-worthiness, features that were warmly welcomed by those whose job it is to fly them. The machine depicted here also features additional armour plating in the cockpit area, with the scabbed-on sheets being clearly visible directly ahead of the forward cabin doorway

Right Full-frontal 'frog'! An unusual but distinctive view of a CH-46E in full battle rig, with 12.7 mm machine guns protruding from both forward cabin doors as well as flare dispensers on the sponsons and infrared jamming devices on the aft rotor housing. As can be seen, the pilot and co-pilot enjoy excellent forward visibility but judging by the amount of daylight visible behind them, this Sea Knight is not carrying much in the way of cargo and it is likely that it has just deposited a cabin-full of troops on a landing zone

Although the Sea Knight seems to spend most of its time at ultra low level, it is no stranger to much higher altitudes and these two views emphatically confirm that the helicopter is equally at home in either situation. A casual glance at the high level study could lead one to believe that these two Sea Knights are engaged in air combat tactics training and that the leading CH-46 is manoeuvring desperately to shake off an opponent seeking to take up the classic six o'clock position for a Sidewinder missile shot. However, even the most ardent helicopter pilot would be forced to concede that the Sea Knight is not designed to mix it in the air-to-air arena and, anyway, it is not compatible with Sidewinder. A far more likely scenario is that the two machines are actually engaged in mountain flying training somewhere in Norway

Contrasting colours and mountainous terrain are certainly much in evidence in these views of operations in Norway, an area that was of prime responsibility for Marine Corps personnel committed to the reinforcement of Europe in accordance with US obligations to NATO. With the Cold War at an end following the collapse of communist states in Eastern Europe, the likelihood of conflict has greatly diminished but Norway has been the locale for further exercises and deployments involving Marine Corps assets during the past couple of years. Even though the Marines seldom bother to apply an appropriate coat of temporary camouflage to their helicopters, it is surprising to note that Arctic clothing does not appear to be worn by any of the troops

Displaying a basically grey overall colour scheme that would clearly be far more relevant to winter operations in Norway, the HMM-263 CH-46E Sea Knight portrayed here looks very much out of place as it embarks paratroops against a backdrop of lush, green vegetation. In this instance, apart from the rather obvious bright red helmet worn by one individual, the battledress in use does at least appear to offer a measure of protection from being observed by unwanted eyes

Boeing Vertol CH-46E

Rotor system: rotor diameter each 50 ft 0 in (16.24 m); rotor disc area, total 3926.99 sq ft (364 82 m²)

Fuselage and tail: length overall, rotors turning 84 ft 4 in (25.40 m) and fuselage 44 ft 10 in (13.66 m); height to top of the rear rotor hub 16 ft 8.5 in (5.09 m); wheel base 24 ft 10 in (7.57 m)

Powerplant: two General Electric T58-GE-16 rated at 1870 shp (1394 kW)

Weights: empty 11,585 lb (5255 kg); maximum take-off 24,300 lb (11,022 kg)

Fuel and load: internal fuel 350 US gal (1323 litres); maximum payload 7000 lb (3175 kg)

Speed: maximum speed at sea level 166 mph (267 km/h); maximum cruising speed at sea level 165 mph (266 km/h)

Range: ferry range 690 miles (1110 km); range with a 2400-lb (1088-kg) payload 633 miles (1019 km)

Performance: maximum rate of climb at sea level 1715 ft (523 m) per minute; service ceiling 9400 ft (2865 m); hovering ceiling 9500 ft (2895 m) in ground effect and 5750 ft (1753 m) out of ground effect

Left The crossed sword, battleaxe and knight's helmet motif on the fin of this CH-46E help to identify it as being assigned to medium helicopter squadron HMM-365 'Sky Knights'. Normally resident at New River, North Carolina, when not embarked, the 'Sky Knights' served as 'core unit' aboard *Iwo Jima* for a tour of duty with the US 6th Fleet in 1990. This particular close up view depicts a Sea Knight crew member taking a more detailed look at the aft main rotor assembly during a routine pre-flight inspection aboard ship

Above The flight deck of USS *Guam* (LPH-9) provides a floating home for seven CH-46Es and a brace of AH-1T SeaCobras while the ship sits at anchor during routine training activity in the Mediterranean. Unusually, no CH-53s are to be seen anywhere on deck but it does not automatically follow that none were embarked, since a typical sea-going squadron will almost invariably include some examples of the four major types of helicopter that presently serve with the Marine Corps. Aš is the case here, though, the dominant type will normally be the highly versatile Sea Knight which is far and away the most numerous helicopter to be found in the Marine inventory

Left Fuel lines trail across the flight deck as a pair of seemingly anonymous Sea Knights undergo 'hot' (rotors running) refuelling while operating in the Mediterranean. The apparent lack of unit insignia and identities on these helicopters is misleading, for they are actually fully marked up in low-contrast black, while the machine nearest to the camera has evidently been fitted with a replacement frame for windows adjacent to the pilot's position

Gloomy skies and uninviting seas such as those in evidence here are not the sort of thing that one traditionally associates with Mediterranean waters but it was winter and even the Cote d'Azur cannot reasonably expect to enjoy sunshine all the year round. Lively activity on the part of deck crew assigned to *Iwo Jima* presaged a fairly hectic launch cycle as the ship despatched a gaggle of HMM-365 Sea Knights which were heading out to 'hit the beach'. Operating off the French coast near Montpellier in early 1990, *Iwo Jima* was one of the key elements committed to *Mayflower*. A joint US-French series of military manoeuvres, *Mayflower* was just one of many exercises that HMM-365 took part in while embarked, such activities enabling Marine aviators to acquire and perfect the kind of skill that is required in the successful conduct of air and sea-borne assault operations

Although Marine Corps helicopter squadrons are usually associated with sea-borne operations, the amount of time that is actually spent aboard ship is relatively insignificant and the service is quick to establish shore facilities at the earliest opportunity. The principal motive behind this is that helicopter operations are adjudged to be far less vulnerable when conducted from a shore base, this being a lesson that was emphatically confirmed when the British ship *Atlantic Conveyor* was destroyed along with several irreplaceable helicopters during the 1982 battle for the Falkland Islands. So, one of the first Marine actions will be to determine the best sites and then occupy them, a process that is depicted here. Inevitably, fuel supplies are a vital need if the service is to undertake sustained operations and this CH-46E from HMM-162 is seen delivering an underslung fuel cell to a forward landing site as a prelude to itself being topped up in readiness for getting back to airlift tasks between ship and shore

Above With weapons at the ready, Marine ground troops – universally known as 'grunts' – fan out from a pair of HMM-162 Sea Knight helicopters at a landing zone during assault training exercises somewhere in Corsica. One of their first actions will normally be that of securing the LZ in readiness for the arrival of a more substantial force that can move out into surrounding countryside and extend the perimeter. Just how seriously these 'grunts' are taking this exercise is difficult to determine, but the absence of helmets seems to indicate that they are not expecting much in the way of opposition from hostile 'blue' forces

Right It really is stating the obvious but one of the most useful features of the helicopter is its ability to land almost anywhere that offers a reasonably level surface as well as one that is free from obstacles. With plenty of experience behind them, the Marines are past masters at finding suitable landing sites and they are also quite adept at getting into locations that are less than ideal, as anyone who saw TV coverage of the evacuation from Saigon will be all too well aware. The crew of this CH-46E seem to have picked a pretty good spot, although they might well be a little peeved when they realise that a photographer succeeded in beating them to it

Although it is perfectly capable of airlifting all sorts of cargo, the CH-46 is probably best known as a troop carrier and Marine Corps operations certainly make plenty of use of its abilities in this respect, using it as an assault vehicle in helping to establish and secure a beach-head as well as a means of enhancing mobility by ferrying troops around a battlefield. In normal configuration, a typical load is some 17 fully-equipped soldiers and this collection of illustrations depicts Sea Knights from HMM-261 rendezvousing with foot soldiers during exercise *Phinia* which took place in Corsica at the beginning of 1989. All three of the Sea Knights shown here appear to be of the latest modification standard, featuring additional armour plate protection adjacent to vulnerable areas such as the cockpit and engines. They are also fitted with flare dispensers and infrared jammers

Left 'Look, no hands.' Three lightly-equipped troops seem to be enjoying their descent as they rappel down to earth from a hovering CH-46 Sea Knight under the eyes of a watching door gunner. The so-called 'hell hole' through which they left the helicopter can be easily seen. Although descents of this type are often practised, holding a hover throughout can obviously result in presenting hostile forces with a fat and juicy target, and it probably would not be all that much fun for anyone on the rappel line either when bullets started whizzing by. However, even though it is preferable to land in order to disgorge troops, this method does allow forces to be inserted into locations where landing zones are hard to find, such as heavily forested areas or in mountainous regions

Above Low-visibility national insignia and other markings and inscriptions are evident in this study of the forward fuselage section of a CH-46E that bears plenty of evidence of touched-up paint work, as well as the nickname 'The Chariot'. Other noteworthy features are the additional armour plating adjacent to the first pilot's seat and the winch that is fitted to the fuselage side directly aft of the cabin doorway. Also of interest is the positioning of the defensive machine gun armament, which makes use of the forward fuselage cut-out that remains following removal of a cabin window, this being a location that is sometimes preferred so as to leave the door free for use by crew members

Above With its rear ramp partially lowered, a CH-46E from HMM-365 taxies out to the lift-off point during intensive operations from Canjuers, while an AH-1T SeaCobra lurks in the background. The distinctive three-tone camouflage scheme applied to many CH-46Es during the latter half of the 1980s is displayed to advantage in this view and there is also evidence that another Sea Knight has surrendered an airframe panel to this machine, as the second letter of the unit tail code clearly does not match up

Right In addition to the rappel technique, another method of inserting troops where a landing is not possible relies on nothing more sophisticated than dangling a strong rope from the ramp at the rear of the Sea Knight. Maintaining a hover this close to trees requires a certain amount of skill on the part of the pilot, but it must call for considerable nerve and one hell of a lot of good old-fashioned muscle power to actually climb down a rope when one is being battered by downwash from the tail rotor

Death Rider

02

HMM-365

G/C

Sgt. S. Velasquez Jr.

 SQUEZ

Above left With tie-down chains securing it firmly to the deck and with rotor blades folded, this Sea Knight clearly is not likely to be going anywhere in a hurry. Assigned to HMM-162 'Golden Eagles', it displays the squadron's motif on the forward rotor fairing, this being flippantly referred to by members of the unit as the 'chicken with sticks', although it is actually meant to portray an eagle. The basically matt green overall colour scheme was universally applied to Marine Corps helicopters for most of the 1970s and 80s, although it has now largely been supplanted by new disruptive types of camouflage pattern

Left The bolted-on armour plating which was added to the Sea Knight is often pressed into service as a form of canvas for squadron artists who are keen to personalise helicopters, and many of the Sea Knights which saw action during the Gulf War did display highly distinctive (and probably highly unofficial) additional markings. The decoration seen here actually predates that conflict by a year or so and was observed and photographed during HMM-365's visit to France in January 1990. Evidently

applied in whitewash, it encapsulates the fascination with motor bikes that is felt by many Americans, although one is inclined to wonder what Harley-Davidson would make of this evidently illicit use of their trade mark by the Sea Knight's crew chief

Above right Sea Knight, Super Stallion and Iroquois helicopters can be seen on the flight deck in this view of *Guadalcanal* as it puts out to sea from a port on the French Mediterranean coast. Typical capacity is somewhere in the region of 20 helicopters although the mix can and often does vary, depending upon the task that is to be undertaken. Usually, though, it is the CH-46 which is the most numerous type, befitting its status as the 'workhorse' of the Marine Corps helicopter fleet. In addition, of course, more potent air power may also be embarked in the form of the AV-8B Harrier II, which is a far from unfamiliar sight aboard vessels of this type, and a large amphibious assault task force may well include one ship with a complement that consists entirely of the V/STOL jet so as to provide a measure of organic air support

Watched by the Sea Knight's loadmaster, deck crew scurry clear with chocks and tie-down chains as a CH-46E from HMM-263 winds up to full power during the NATO exercise *Team Work 92*. Then, flying from *Guadalcanal*, the squadron took part in a major amphibious operation in Norway and many of its helicopters donned an unusual grey overall colour scheme which was found to be particularly effective in the Arctic environment. This machine was perhaps untypical in that it seems to have been subjected to more than its fair share of patching

Arguably the most attractive finish yet to be seen applied to the Sea Knight, the grey overall colour scheme is portrayed here in action on a couple of different CH-46Es from HMM-263 during the unit's 1992 deployment in Norway. Minor differences can be discerned in the presentation of the unit code letters on the tail rotor housing, but otherwise the markings applied to this pair of helicopters appear to conform very closely in style and location. In the early years of service, an overall glossy green finish was applied across the fleet, in concert with white titles and a full-colour 'star and bar', but these were progressively toned-down in the late 1970s when a switch was made to matt green overall with black titles and national insignia as depicted in some of the accompanying illustrations. More recently, the disruptive pattern of grey, black and green has been the most widely used scheme but quite a few Sea Knights also adopted desert camouflage for the duration of *Desert Shield* and *Desert Storm*. As a result of all these colour variations, about the only thing that can be said with any degree of certainty is that we have not yet seen all the colour schemes that will be applied to the Sea Knight during its career with the Marine Corps

Left Looking almost lost against an imposing mountain backdrop, an HMM-263 Sea Knight heads towards the sanctuary of its parent ship during manoeuvres in Norway. Below it, the tranquillity of the mirror-like surface of the fjord is disturbed by the faintest of ripples, with only the helicopter intruding upon what is otherwise a virtually timeless scene

Above Dwarfed by the tank landing ship USS *La Moure County*, amphibious assault craft scurry to and fro between ship and shore during an exercise in the close confines of Norway's Malaven fjord while a gaggle of Marine Corps helicopters thrash their way down a valley that is bounded by snow-capped and mist-shrouded mountains. Examples of the troop-carrying CH-53E Super Stallion and CH-46E Sea Knight are shepherded by a brace of AH-1W SuperCobras as they approach the landing zone, and the gunships will almost certainly maintain a watching brief during the period of greatest vulnerability while the larger helicopters are sitting idle on the ground as they offload. Meanwhile, other more potent Marine Corps air power will not be far away, with fighters like the F/A-18 Hornet being tasked to furnish top cover for the landing

Modernisation of the Sea Knight helicopter certainly did not cease with delivery of the remanufactured CH-46E version, and this is currently being updated still further so as to ensure that the Boeing-Vertol creation continues in service with the Marines until such time as a replacement becomes available. Whether that replacement will be Sikorsky's S-92 or, as the Marines would prefer, the V-22 Osprey remains to be seen. For the moment though, the Sea Knight reins supreme, and its latest guise as the CH-46E 'Bullfrog' has resulted in it acquiring flotation gear in bulky containers adjacent to the centre fuselage section, while it also features additional fuel capacity in the much enlarged sponsons that house the main undercarriage members. One of the first Fleet Marine Force Atlantic squadrons to obtain the 'Bullfrog' was HMM-162, and a modified CH-46E from this unit is portrayed here during the *Display Determination 91* exercise when undertaking cross-deck operations from the French amphibious vessel *La Foudre*

Left Like most military forces, the Marines are not adverse to plastering their hardware with eye-catching and often lurid artwork, such decorative additions certainly not being confined to the world of the fast jet fraternity. Another instance of helicopter decoration is provided by this HMM-162 CH-46E 'Bullfrog', which displays a scantily clad redhead clutching a shield and sword as she rides a decidedly ferocious looking polar bear into action. Below her, the two crew members look bored to the point of distraction as they await a fresh task

Right While most of the Sea Knight's applications are concerned with combat, it has frequently been called upon to fulfil humanitarian functions, and the capacious cabin is well suited to the movement of food supplies and the evacuation of civilians. These are tasks which have often been undertaken by Marine helicopter squadrons, with one of the most recent instances of the 'Flying Leathernecks' being called upon to engage in disaster relief work centering around Kurdistan. In April 1991, during operation *Provide Comfort*, Marine helicopters were quickly in action, airlifting Kurdish refugees to areas far removed from Saddam Hussein's reach and also ferrying life-saving supplies to the hurriedly created camps. One of the Sea Knights involved in this emergency relief work is seen here being refuelled at a forward operating location somewhere in Turkey *(Photograph by Patrick Allen)*

At least nine Sea Knights, four Super Stallions and an Iroquois can be seen on the flight deck of *Guadalcanal* as it ventures seawards after a brief liberty call in the south of France. Although not possessing anything like the majestic bulk of the Navy's truly massive 'flat tops', these carriers are still fairly imposing vessels. The box-like structure situated directly in front of the island is one of two Sea Sparrow BPDMS (Basic Point Defence Missile System) launchers, with other defensive kit comprising the Vulcan Phalanx CIWS (Close In Weapon System), which is fundamentally a radar-directed multi-barrelled 20 mm cannon. As with BPDMS, two of these weapons are installed, the starboard device being visible below the Sea Sparrow launcher

Marine Corps operation of the Sea Knight is by no means confined to the medium lift role, for the service also employs a number of suitably modified machines on search and rescue duties. Undernose searchlights and winches are among the more interesting facets of the HH-46D version, but the main identifying feature is the special blue and red colour scheme, which is modelled here by a Sea Knight from Cherry Point's Station Operations and Maintenance Squadron. Functioning as a base flight, the SOMS undertakes routine liaison and communications duties and is also tasked with provision of local crash rescue cover, a mission which on some stations is performed by similarly marked UH-1Ns. Regardless of type, the number of helicopters assigned to a particular SOMS seldom exceeds three, which is sufficient to allow one to be held at near instant readiness, another to be held in reserve and yet another to undergo maintenance

The veteran Huey

Left Bell's Iroquois is arguably the most successful helicopter of all time and a machine which, like the fabled Douglas Dakota, looks as if it might well go on for ever. Marine Corps association with this rotary-winged craft extends over three decades, with the initial contract for the single-engined UH-1E being awarded way back in 1962 and deliveries starting in February 1964. At that time, it was viewed as primarily a light reconnaissance and utility helicopter, but it has since done just about everything from hauling cargo through armed escort to the evacuation of casualties from the field of battle. Today, the UH-1E no longer figures in the inventory and the standard model is the UH-1N, an example of which is shown here over desert terrain in the western United States

Below With its grey overall paint job showing much evidence of hasty attempts at patching up, a UH-1N of composite squadron HMM-365 hover taxies to a landing site at Canjuers during operations from *Iwo Jima* in early 1990. Close study of the landing skids reveals that additional radio equipment seems to have been temporarily attached to the front fuselage attachment members, and it is likely that this particular Iroquois was being used in a command and control capacity for exercise *Mayflower 90*

Above Wearing a basically green camouflage colour scheme which provides a striking contrast to the all-grey example portrayed previously, another UH-1N from HMM-365 proceeds cautiously at ultra low level during a nap-of-earth flight exercise. Cabin crew members assist with look-out and close study of this particular Huey reveals a number of differences when compared with other examples illustrated in this chapter. Most obvious is the presence of a rocket pod on the weapons rack and it also features an infra-red jammer, although no protection is provided to counter the risk of a wire strike

Left Apparently undisturbed by the noisy departure of a CH-46E 'frog', Marine Corps personnel gather by the open cabin of an HMM-365 Huey at Canjuers for a briefing on the operational area over which they will shortly be flying. Features of interest on this rather shabby UH-1N include weapons racks adjacent to the cabin, a flare dispenser unit on the tail boom directly ahead of the low-visibility national insignia and wire-cutting devices above and below the cockpit

Above Perched somewhat precariously in the open doorway of a UH-1N, a gunner lets rip with his pintle-mounted M-60 7.62 mm machine gun during a live firing exercise, while a colleague ensures that the ammunition belt feeds correctly into the weapon. Aiming clearly relies on nothing more sophisticated than aligning front and rear sights on a target before blazing away and no attempt is made to prevent littering the countryside with spent cartridge cases, some of which can be seen tumbling away into space

Right Flightdeck crew of the *Austin* Class amphibious transport dock USS *Nashville* (LPD-13) watch a rather anonymous looking UH-1N Iroquois as it sinks to a landing somewhere in Mediterranean waters. Known as LPDs, vessels like the *Nashville* have only a modest aviation support capability, with facilities being limited to the landing platform shown here and a telescopic hangar, track-way associated with the latter being visible to the left. Two of the 12-strong class, including the *Nashville*, have been configured to serve as flagships and this visiting Huey could conceivably be in use as a kind of airborne 'Admiral's barge'

Although it is the machines which constitute the main subject of this volume, one should never forget that they are unable to function without man's input and these two views show Marine Corps personnel in very different situations. Ceremonial occasions provide opportunities to bring out flags and banners, but this one does not seem to have gone totally overboard with regard to 'spit and polish' and normal battledress seems to be the order of the day. Combat fatigues are also much in evidence in the second view, which shows ground troops relaxing as they await the order to 'ship out' aboard some of the adjacent helicopters. Camouflage paint is certainly much in evidence and one or two of these individuals have possibly been a shade too enthusiastic in applying it, although the soldier in the lower left might well have turned green through fear of flying!

Bell UH-1N

Rotor system: main rotor diameter with tracking tips 48 ft 2.25 in (14.69 m); tail rotor diameter 8 ft 6 in (2.59 m); main rotor disc area 1823.72 sq ft (169.42 m²); tail rotor disc area 56.74 sq ft (5.27 m²)

Fuselage and tail: length overall, rotors turning 57 ft 3.25 in (17.46 m) and fuselage 42 ft 4.75 in (12.92 m); height 14 ft 4.75 in (4.39 m); tailplane span 9 ft 4.5 in (2.86 m)

Powerplant: one Pratt & Whitney Canada T400-CP-400 rated at 1800 shp (1342 kW) but flat rated to 1290 shp (962 kW) for take-off and 1100 shp (820 kW) for continuous running

Weights: empty 6196 lbs (2798 kg); normal take-off 10,500 lbs (4762 kg); maximum take-off 11,200 lb (5080 kg)

Fuel and load: internal fuel 215 US gal (814 litres); maximum payload 3383 lb (1534 kg)

Speed: maximum level speed at sea level 126 mph (203 km/h)

Range: maximum range 248 miles (400 km)

Performance: maximum rate of climb at sea level 1745 ft (532 m) per minute; service ceiling 15,000 ft (4570 m); hovering ceiling 12,900 ft (3930 m) in ground effect and 4900 ft (1495 m) out of ground effect

Left A munitions specialist goes about the task of arming a seven-round rocket launcher pod affixed to the starboard weapons rack of a UH-1N Iroquois. Although it lacks the ability to operate with precision munitions such as those employed by the AH-1, the Huey can still pack a fairly powerful punch and is more than capable of spoiling the day of anyone unlucky or unwise enough to be in the impact area of a salvo of 2.75 in rockets like these

Above At first glance, it seems as though the Huey crewman is offering a Masonic handshake but a closer look reveals that he is actually straightening out his intercom lead. The 'YS' code combination on the tail rotor mast signifies that this UH-1N is operating with HMM-162, which served as 'core unit' for a recent deployment aboard the USS *Wasp* (LHD-1). Composite squadrons are usually organised with the task very much in mind and generally feature a preponderance of medium-lift CH-46 Sea Knight or heavy-lift CH-53 Stallion helicopters. As a consequence, it is rare for the number of Hueys attached to such a unit to exceed four or five

Desert Shield

Almost inevitably, the Marines had a vital part to play in the efforts to liberate Kuwait and the service duly despatched more than 300 helicopters to the war zone for *Desert Shield* and *Desert Storm*, assigning these to four Marine Aircraft Groups for the duration. Operations were conducted from land and sea bases, with the assembly of a substantial amphibious force being a key factor in misleading Iraqi intelligence experts as to the nature of coalition intentions when the ground war began in earnest in late February. Heavy-lift resources were drawn from a total of eight squadrons, which between them mustered some 75 examples of the CH-53D, RH-53D and CH-53E. This is a CH-53D Sea Stallion from HMH-463 which was one of several Fleet Marine Force Pacific units that were assigned to MAG-16. Although some Sea Stallions and Super Stallions were given desert camouflage, this particular example retains a temperate finish

Missions undertaken by Sikorsky's heavyweight covered pretty much the entire range of airlift duties, with the CH-53 being called upon to move men and material around the vastness of the Saudi Arabian desert during the build-up to full-scale war. Frequently operating from remote landing sites, excessive heat and the almost ever present clouds of swirling sand and dust made routine operations difficult and presented maintenance troops with an unenviable task as they strove to keep their charges mission ready. This sequence of pictures, portraying CH-53Ds of HMH-463 collecting troops from a desert outpost, illustrates well the kind of landing zones that were used. Two other regular squadrons also despatched CH-53Ds to the Gulf, where this model was slightly outnumbered by the three-engined CH-53E Super Stallion which was flown by four squadrons. In addition, a few RH-53Ds from a reserve unit at Alameda were also present

Contrasting colours are evident in this view of a CH-53D and a CH-46E at one of the more permanent operating bases used by Marine Corps helicopter units. Although they were often escorted by heavily-armed gunships, both types did make some concessions to the fact that they were active in a potential war zone by employing a variety of defensive countermeasures kit. Flare dispensers are certainly fitted to the two helicopters seen here, these being scabbed on to the aft fuselage side of the CH-53D and mounted on top of the sponson of the CH-46E. In addition, 7.62 mm machine guns were also fitted as standard, in the event of suppressive fire being required for any reason. So as to keep the rear ramps clear for loading and off loading, gunners were usually situated in the forward doorway of both types, to port and starboard

One of the principal operating bases for Marine Corps helicopters was located in the King Abdul Aziz naval base complex at Al Jubail, where a suitably-camouflaged CH-46E Sea Knight from medium helicopter squadron HMM-165 is seen receiving attention to the innards of its forward rotor pylon. Judging by the rather pained expression on the face of one of the mechanics, something is proving rather difficult to shift, an observation that was equally applicable to Saddam Hussein, although it was not quite so relevant to his Army, which did not take much persuasion to depart from Kuwait when the ground war started. Other Marine Corps helicopter types that flew from King Abdul Aziz comprised the AH-1W SuperCobra, UH-1N Iroquois and CH-53 Stallion, with by far the greater majority of the 180-odd land-based machines being nominally stationed here during the build-up, while another 140 or so operated from ships such as *Guam, Iwo Jima, New Orleans* (LPH-11), *Okinawa* (LPH-3) and *Tarawa* (LHA-1), which were cruising the waters of the nearby Gulf

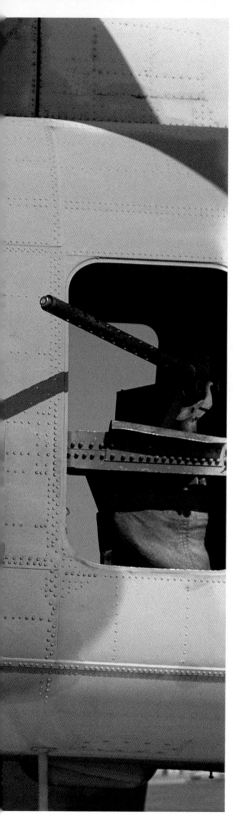

Inscriptions on the access platform adjacent to this CH-46E Sea Knight would appear to indicate that this item of equipment was actually owned by the Kuwait Air Force but just how it found its way to the airfield at Dhahran is probably as mysterious as the way in which some airport baggage trolleys keep turning up in the most unlikely places. Regardless of that, there is evidence that it was being put to good use in returning this HMM-161 helicopter to flight status. A closer examination of the above picture reveals that a flare dispenser is attached to the sponson and the tail rotor mast also features an infrared jammer, while more lethal defensive equipment includes the 7.62 mm machine gun that can be seen protruding from the forward cabin doorway in the close-up photograph *(Both photographs by Ian Black)*

Although the exploits of the Army's AH-64A Apache and the Air Force's A-10A in the tank-killing business received a considerable amount of publicity, the Marine Corps also made a solid contribution when it came to eliminating the threat posed by Iraqi armoured fighting vehicles. Much of the credit for that correctly belongs to ground echelons, but the SuperCobra was also heavily committed to action, with four of the six units that operate this potent helicopter despatching men and machines to the Gulf. The AH-1W shown here in a temperate camouflage colour scheme is from HMLA-269, which initially flew from Dhahran, Saudi Arabia, where it was photographed during the build-up. This squadron subsequently embarked its AH-1Ws and UH-1Ns aboard ships of the 4th Marine Expeditionary Brigade shortly before *Desert Storm* blew up

Another squadron which despatched SuperCobra and Iroquois helicopters to the Gulf was HMLA-369, which is normally resident at Camp Pendleton, California. Unlike HMLA-269, however, this unit remained ashore at Al Jubail for the duration of its tour of duty and it also took the opportunity to give its helicopters a more appropriate camouflage finish. The AH-1W portrayed here may well have been caught by the camera before repainting was completed, for it is unusual in featuring a basically sand overall colour scheme. It is also all but anonymous, with the only visual identification marking consisting of a three-digit code number on the forward fuselage. Even though it carries no external armament, it is fitted with launch rails for the Hellfire anti-armour missile, another slightly more unusual feature being the addition of fine mesh filters to reduce the risk of sand and dust ingestion

Above Munitions specialists at Dhahran prepare to extract a Hellfire anti-armour missile from its shipping container prior to arming an AH-1W SuperCobra of HMLA-269. In combat, Marine Corps AH-1s employed TOW as the principal tank-busting weapon, presumably because this missile does not require its target to be illuminated by laser. When Hellfire was used, designation was evidently undertaken by ground forces in scout vehicles. Although some of the four squadrons which deployed with the AH-1W applied desert camouflage to their machines, HMLA-269 seems to have left most of its gunships in a temperate scheme, such as that seen here on the appropriately named 'Lizard King' *(Photograph by Ian Black)*

Right Another variation of desert camouflage is worn by this HMLA-369 SuperCobra as it receives attention from mechanics at its desert base during the lead-up to war. Again, apart from a code number, there is little evidence of unit assignment, but it does at least display the familiar 'star and bar' national insignia, part of which can just be discerned below the forward edge of the stub wing. It also carries the AH-1W designation at the base of the tail rotor fairing but there is no sign of a serial number anywhere on the exterior of this machine

Above With cockpit instruments and controls shrouded against the fierce Saudi Arabian sun, an AH-1W of HMLA-369 is readied for flight by ground crew as a UH-1N comes in to land in the distance. TOW launch tubes and sand filters are in evidence on this machine and one of the two SuperCobras visible in the background is also fitted with the latter, even though it and the neighbouring machine are incapable of flight by virtue of lacking tail rotors

Left A technician explores the innards of the engine compartment on one of the 80 or so Marine Corps Cobra gunships that were despatched to the Gulf region for *Desert Shield* and *Desert Storm* while its pilot waits patiently for an opportunity to get airborne once the work is completed. This photograph was taken soon after HMLA-369 arrived in the Gulf in September 1990 while their AH-1Ws and UH-1Ns were being restored to full air worthiness. This machine carries just a two-round TOW missile fit and lacks flare dispenser equipment

A gaggle of AH-1W SuperCobras launch from their Saudi base at Al Jubail at the start of yet another training sortie over inhospitable desert terrain during the tense period that preceded full-scale combat operations. Three-digit code numbers in a different numerical sequence and a rather distinctive blue/grey camouflage indicate that these AH-1W SuperCobras were assigned to HMLA-367 at Camp Pendleton, which was one of the pair of light attack helicopter squadrons that flew with Marine Aircraft Group 16. Closer examination reveals that different weapons provisions were made, with both TOW and Hellfire missile launch systems in use, although no armament was being carried by these helicopters

Above Even though it might in some ways figure as the most versatile helicopter ever to have seen service with the Marines, the UH-1N was actually present in fewer numbers than other rotary wing types during *Desert Shield* and *Desert Storm,* with approximately 50 being despatched to the Gulf. As with other helicopters, these employed a variety of different colour schemes, those assigned to HMLA-369 being painted in similar fashion to the much more warlike SuperCobras of this squadron

Above and below left Evidence of the ever increasing probability of war is provided by the fact that the HMLA-369 Hueys shown coming and going from the main operating base at Al Jubail have been fitted with M-60 machine gun armament. Although they did undertake some routine communications and liaison duties while in the Gulf, the primary role of the Marine Corps UH-1N was one of supporting the formidable AH-1W SuperCobra once the fighting started in January. This was mainly accomplished by scouting for targets, but it is also likely that the Huey was used to carry extra TOW missiles so that the SuperCobras could make use of forward area refuelling and rearming points at remote desert sites close to the battlefield

Door gunners in the leading Huey keep an anxious eye on the surface of the desert floor as their helicopter sweeps in to land at a forward location somewhere in Saudi Arabia. This brace of UH-1Ns are from HMLA-367, which was one of four frontline light attack helicopter squadrons that operated Hueys in *Desert Shield*. In addition, one Huey-equipped Reserve Force outfit also saw action during the build-up and the war, specifically HML-767 which deployed from New Orleans, Louisiana, to the King Abdul Aziz military complex at Al Jubail, where it operated alongside elements of the Fleet Marine Force Atlantic as part of Marine Aircraft Group 26

Marine Helicopter Squadrons

Regular-force Marine Helicopter Squadrons, Heavy

Number	Code	Base	Equipment
HMH-361 'Pineapples'	YN	Tustin, Ca	CH-53E
HMH-362 'Ugly Angels'	YL	New River, NC	CH-53D
HMH-363 'Red Lions'	YZ	Tustin, Ca	CH-53D
HMH-461 'Sea Stallions'	CJ	New River, NC	CH-53E
HMH-462 'Heavy Haulers'	YF	Tustin, Ca	CH-53D
HMH-463	YH	Kaneohe Bay, Hi	CH-53D
HMH-464 'Condors'	EN	New River, NC	CH-53E
HMH-465 'Warhorses'	YJ	Tustin, Ca	CH-53E
HMH-466	YK	Tustin, Ca	CH-53E

Regular-force Marine Helicopter Attack Squadrons, Light

Number	Code	Base	Equipment
HMLA-167	TV	New River, NC	AH-1W, UH-1N
HMLA-169 'Vipers'	SN	Camp Pendelton, Ca	AH-1W, UH-1N
HMLA-267 'Black Aces'	UV	Camp Pendelton, Ca	AH-1W, UH-1N
HMLA-269 'Sea Cobras'	HF	New River, NC	AH-1W, UH-1N
HMLA-367 'Scarface'	VT	Camp Pendelton, Ca	AH-1W, UH-1N
HMLA-369 'Gunfighters'	SM	Camp Pendelton, Ca	AH-1W, UH-1N

Regular-force Marine Helicopter Squadrons, Medium

Number	Code	Base	Equipment
HMM-161	YR	Tustin, Ca	CH-46E
HMM-162 'Golden Eagles'	YS	New River, NC	CH-46E
HMM-163 'Ridgerunners'	YP	Tustin, Ca	CH-46E
HMM-164 'Knightriders'	YT	Tustin, Ca	CH-46E
HMM-165	YW	Kaneohe Bay, Hi	CH-46E
HMM-166 'Sea Elks'	YX	Tustin, Ca	CH-46E
HMM-261	EM	New River, NC	CH-46E
HMM-262 'Flying Tigers'	ET	Kaneohe Bay, Hi	CH-46E
HMM-263	EG	New River, NC	CH-46E
HMM-264	EH	New River, NC	CH-46E
HMM-265	EP	Kaneohe Bay, Hi	CH-46E
HMM-266 'Griffins'	ES	New River, NC	CH-46E
HMM-268	YQ	Tustin, Ca	CH-46E
HMM-364	PF	Kaneohe Bay, Hi	CH-46E
HMM-365 'Sky Knights'	YM	New River, NC	CH-46E

Regular-force Marine Helicopter Training Squadrons

Number	Code	Base	Equipment
HMT-204	GX	New River, NC	CH-46E
HMT-301	SU	Tustin, Ca	CH-46E
HMT-302	UT	Tustin, Ca	CH-53D/E
HMT-303	QT	Camp Pendelton, Ca	AH-1W, UH-1N

Regular-force Experimental Helicopter Squadron

Number	Code	Base	Equipment
HMX-1	MX	Quantico, Va	CH/VH-53D, VH-3D, VH-46F, VH-60N, CH-46E

Base SAR Flights

Location	Code	Equipment
Beaufort, SC	5B	HH-46D
Cherry Point, SC	5C	HH-46D
El Toro, Ca	5T	HH-1N
Iwakuni, Japan	5G	HH-46D
Kaneohe Bay, Hi	KB	HH-46D
Yuma, Az	5Y	HH-1N

Reserve-force Helicopter Squadrons, Attack

Number	Code	Base	Equipment
HMA-773 'Cobras'	MP	Atlanta, Ga	AH-1J/W
HMA-775 'Coyotes'	WR	Camp Pendelton, Ca	AH-1J/W

Reserve-force Helicopter Squadrons, Heavy

HMH-772	MT	Willow Grove, Pa	CH-53D
HMH-772 Det A	MS	Alameda, Ca	RH-53D
HMH-772 Det B	QM	Dallas, Tx	CH-53D

Reserve-force Helicopter Squadrons, Light

HML-767	MM	New Orleans, La	UH-1N
HML-771	QK	South Weymouth, Ma	UH-1N
HML-776	QL	Glenview, Il	UH-1N

Reserve-force Helicopter Squadrons, Medium

HMM-764	ML	Tustin, Ca	CH-46E
HMM-774	MQ	Norfolk, Va	CH-46E

NOTE – Although code combinations are assigned to all units, these are not necessarily always applied to helicopters. Instances of this are provided by some FMFPac HMLA squadrons and by helicopters allocated to base SAR elements.